THE TALE OF ANNALEE AND HER KITTEN DIEGO.

ANNALEE WAS A LITTLE GIRL WHO ALWAYS PLAYED ALONE BECAUSE SHE WAS AN ONLY CHILD AND OF COURSE SOMETIMES HER TWO UNCLES WOULD PLAY WITH HER, WHETHER IT WAS BUILDING THINGS, OR EVEN JUST USING THEIR IMAGINATIONS. AND BOY DID LITTLE ANNA LOVE HER UNCLES MORE THAN ANYTHING IN THE WORLD, BUT EVEN THOUGH SHE LOVED THEM, ANNA NEEDED A LITTLE SOMETHING MORE THAN JUST HER UNCLES TO PLAY WITH. SHE NEEDED A FRIEND THAT SHE

COULD TALK TO WHENEVER SHE WAS SAD, MAD OR EVEN GLAD BECAUSE HER TWO UNCLES WERE NOT ALWAYS AROUND AND THEY BOTH HAD JOBS. ONE UNCLE WORKED TWO JOBS AND THE OTHER WAS AN AUTHOR WHO LOVED TELLING STORIES, ONE OF WHICH HE EVEN LET ANNA LEE HELP HIM WITH.

SHE WAS ONLY 4 YEARS OLD SO SOME DAYS SHE WANTED TO GROW OLDER AND BECOME A COP THEN OTHER DAYS SHE SAID SHE WANTED TO BE A DOCTOR, BUT IT JUST SO HAPPENED ANNA WANTED TO BE A FAMOUS AUTHOR THE DAY HER UNCLE AUSTIN LET HER HELP HIM WRITE HER VERRY

FIRST BOOK.

LETS WRITE
ABOUT DIEGO!!!

WHEN ANNA WAS HAPPY, SHE HAD A SMILE THAT LIT UP EVERYTHING AROUND HER. EVEN WHEN SHE WAS LONELY, THERE WAS STILL A LIGHT SHINING DEEP WITHIN HER AND REFLECTED ON OTHERS. AND ONE DAY THIS POWERFUL LIGHT OF HERS GLEAMED WITH PURE HAPPINESS, WHEN SUDDENLY A BABY KITTEN APPEARED OUTSIDE OF ANNA'S BEDROOM DOOR ONE SPECIAL NIGHT.

ONLY A SCRATCH AND A PURR WERE ABLE TO AWAKEN ANNA WITH NOT EVEN A BLUR. SHE GOT OUT OF BED AND LOOKED UNDER THE DOOR, HOPING TO SEE WHAT SHE SAW BEFORE, A MOUSE UNDER HER DOOR AS THE CLOCK STRUCK 4:00, OR MAYBE IT WAS HER GRANDMA WITH SOME MILK THAT WAS WARMER THAN WARM. BUT WHEN ANNA TURNED THE KNOB EVER SO SLOWLY AND OPENED THE DOOR, IT WAS NOT HER GRANDMA WITH A GLASS OF MILK, OR EVEN A MOUSE THAT SHE SEEN BEFORE. BUT A KITTEN WITH A PURR LOOKING UP AT HER, SMILING A SMILE THAT ANNA HAS NEVER SEEN BEFORE. THEY BOTH STAIRED AT EACH OTHER FOR A MOMENT CLASHING SMILING LIGHTS, THEN THE KITTEN SPOKE "MY NAME IS DIEGO; CAN I BE YOUR FRIEND?" ANNA LOOKED AMAZED WITH THAT LOOK ON

HER FACE AS IF SHE WERE DREAMING A DREAM ONLY SHE WISHED WAS REAL.

YES, I HAVE ALWAYS WANTED A FRIEND SHE SAID WITH EXCITEMENT!!! PICKING DIEGO UP IN HER ARMS LIKE A CHARM THAT NOBODY CAN HARM, AND KISSING DIEGO ON HIS FOREHEAD AS THEY BOTH JUMPED IN TO BED. GOOD NIGHT MY FRIEND ANNA SAID FALLING INTO A DEEP SLEEP.

WAKING UP THE NEXT MORNING TO DIEGO LICKING HER FACE, ANNA REALIZED IT WAS NEVER A DREAM AFTER ALL, THEN ANNA'S GRANDMA JEANETTE WALKED INTO THE ROOM WITH NOT EVEN A SOUND, PULLING THE COVERS DOWN TO FIND ANNA PRETENDING TO SLEEP WITH NOT EVEN A PEEP, WAKEUP MY DEAR I AM HOME, AND I'VE MISSED YOU SHE SAID, HUGGING ANNA TIGHTLY THEN KISSING HER EVER SO SLIGHTLY ON HER FOREHEAD, WHILE TURNING TO THE

MIRROR FOR A QUICK GLANCE...

ANNA LEE OPENED HER EYES TO DISCOVER THERE WAS NO KITTEN IN SIGHT AND SUDDENLY CRIED. DO NOT CRY MY LOVE HER GRANDMOTHER SAID, BUT MY NEW FRIEND IS GONE OUT OF MY BED. YOU MUST OF BEN DREAMING, I WILL FIND YOU A FRIEND. NO, I WANT DIEGO MY KITTEN INSTEAD. WE DO NOT HAVE A KITTEN OR EVEN A MOUSE IT IS ALL IN YOUR DREAMS SO THERE IS NOTHING TO WORRY ABOUT, ANNA'S GRANDMA JEANNETTE SAID. BUT HE WAS JUST HEAR A MINUTE AGO BEFORE YOU WALKED IN MY ROOM LITTLE ANNA LEE REPLIED WITH A TEAR BUILDING UP IN THE CORNER OF HER EYE. EVERYTHING IS GOING TO BE ALRIGHT HER GRANDMA SAID, IF I AM HERE YOU WILL BE FINE. THAN ANNA'S SADNESS TURNED TO

HAPPINESS AND WHAT WAS ONCE A TEAR QUICKLY TURNED IN TO A SHINE WITH A BIG SMILE AS SHE SAW DIEGO HIDING BEHIND HER BED IN A BASKET WHEN HER GRANDMA TURNED AWAY.

THANK GOODNESS I WASNT DREAMING AFTER ALL

I THOUGHT YOU WERE JUST A DREAM ANNA SAID. OH, BUT I CAN BE WHATEVER IT IS YOU WANT ME TO BE DIEGO SAID. SO, YOU ARE NOT REAL? ANNA ASKED, I AM AS REAL AS YOU SEE ME TO BE DIEGO SAID WITH A MEOW AND A PURR RUBBING HIS HEAD AGAINST ANNA LEE'S RIGHT CHEEK. YOU FEEL REAL AND YOU LOOK REAL, SO YOU ARE REAL TO ME, BOTH LITTLE ANNA LEE AND HER KITTEN DIEGO WENT OUT INTO THE KITCHEN WHERE HER GRANDMA STOOD AT THE COUNTER MAKING HER LUNCH FOR HER FIRST DAY OF HEAD START, CAN YOU MAKE ME TWO LUNCHES GRANDMA, MY TUMMY IS HUNGRY, I PROMISE I WILL EAT IT ALL ANNA SAID WITH A FUNNY LIP.

OH, OK ANNA I GUESS I COULD MAKE YOU TWO LUNCHES BUT YOU MUST EAT YOUR VEGGIES, THEY ARE VERRY NUTRITIOUS FOR YOU AND PROVIDE LOTS OF VITAMINS SO YOU CAN BE STRONG AND HEALTHY, YES!!! OK GRANDMA I WILL EAT ALL MY VEGGIES. GOOD GIRL NOW, GO GET YOUR SOCKS AND SHOES ON AND I WILL HAVE ALL OF YOUR FAVORITES READY TO GO FOR YOU. STRING CHEESE? YES HONEY. CHOCOLATE PUDDING TO? YES BUT ONLY ONE, TO MUCH SUGAR IS NOT GOOD FOR YOU SWEETHEART. DID YOU REMEMBER TO PACK ME TWO YOGURTS? YES, BUT I CAN ONLY PACK YOU ONE YOGURT, REMEMBER YOGURT HAS SUGAR IN IT TO. OK GRANDMA, ANNA SAID WITH A SMILE. WHAT DO YOU SAY BEAUTIFUL? THANKYOU ANNA REPLIED. YOU ARE VERY WELCOME.

THE SCHOOL BUS PULLED UP OUTSIDE OF THE HOUSE AND ANNA GOT ON WITH DIEGO HIDDEN UNDER HER SHIRT. AS THEY REACHED THE SCHOOL ANNA RAN FOR THE PLAYGROUND TO BE ALONE WITH HER NEW FRIEND, BUT THERE WAS A BIG BULLY, GARTH, WHO KEPT POKING HER IN THE ARM AND TRYING TO GRAB HER KITTEN SO DO YOU KNOW WHAT ANNA LEE DID, SHE STOOD UP FOR HERSELF AND TOLD GARTH, THE BULLY TO PLEASE LEAVE HER ALONE OR SHE WAS GOING TO TELL THE TEACHER AND THAT WAS BRAVE OF HER.

EVERYBODY SHOULD STAND UP FOR THEM SELF'S AND IT IS NOT NICE TO BULLY OTHERS, SO REMEMBER THAT AND REMEMBER HOW ANNA LEE STOOD UP FOR HERSELF, BECAUSE IT IS IMPORTANT TO NOT LET ANYBODY PICK ON YOU NO MATTER WHAT YOU LOOK LIKE OR WHO YOU ARE BECAUSE WE ARE ALL BEAUTIFUL IN OUR OWN LITTLE WAYS AND WE ALL CARRY THE KEY TO OUR HEARTS LOCKED SAFE.

THE NEXT DAY WHEN THE SCHOOL BUS PULLED UP TO THE SCHOOL AFTER WHAT FELT LIKE HOURS OF SITTING, ANNA TOOK DIEGO AND LEFT THE SCHOOL BUS WITH HER HEART ON HER SLEEVE, FULL OF EXCITEMENT THEY WALKED ONLY TO FIND THEM SELF'S IN A BIT OF A PICKLE, SHE DIDN'T KNOW WHICH CLASS ROOM WAS HERS SINCE SHE SPENT ALL THE DAY BEFORE IN

THE FUN ROOM WITH DIEGO , SO THEY WALKED AROUND TRYING TO FIND HER CLASS, UNTIL THEY CAME UPON A BIG FIELD AND OVER THE OTHER SIDE OF THIS FIELD SAT GIANT SWINGS AND HUMUNGOUS TEETERTOTTERS, WITH ANNA'S FAVORITE RIDE THE SLIDE.

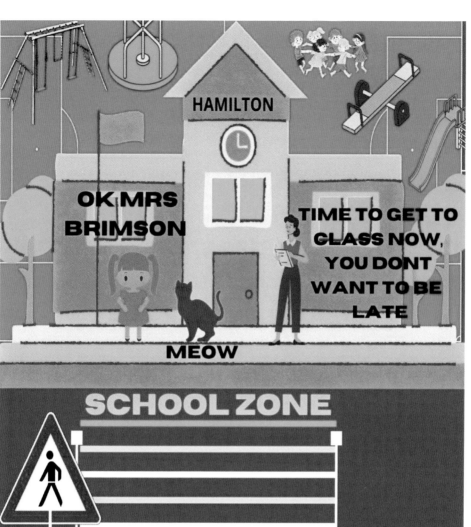

SHE PUT DIEGO DOWN AND THEY BOTH RAN FREELY TO THE PLAYGROUND WHERE THEY LAUGHED SANG AND HAD FUN, IT WAS THE HAPPIEST TIME IN ANNA LEE'S LIFE, SHE FOUND HER VERRY OWN FRIEND THAT SHE COULD TALK TO WHENEVER SHE WAS DOWN AT TIMES, BUT THAT WAS THE THING, SHE WAS NEVER SAD ANYMORE AFTER SHE FOUND HER COMPANION DIEGO.

AND EVEN THOUGH ANNA LEE MADE A FRIEND SHE STILL PLAYED WITH BOTH OF HER UNCLES AND HER GRANDMA AND SHE LOVED THEM JUST AS MUCH AS THEY LOVED HER,

THERE WAS A LOT ANNA LEARNED FROM ALL OF THESE THINGS SHE'S WENT THROUGH, ANNA HAS GAINED SELF CONFIDENCE IN HERSELF AND AS FAR AS FRIENDS GO DIEGO IS AND ALWAYS WILL BE HER BEST FRIEND FOR LIFE, YOU SEE IT DOESN'T MATTER IF YOUR BEST FRIEND IS A DOG, CAT, RHINO OR HIPPO, AT THE END OF THE DAY A FRIEND IS SOMEBODY WHO ACCEPTS US FOR WHO WE ARE REGARDLESS OF OUR DOWNFALLS AND THAT'S EXACTLY WHAT DIEGO WAS TO ANNA.

ANNA LEARNED THAT IT DOESN'T MATTER WHO YOUR FRIENDS ARE AS LONG AS THEY CARE ABOUT YOU AND ONLY WISH THE BEST FOR YOU, SHE ALSO LEARNED THAT YOU DON'T HAVE TO BE AFRAID OF ANYTHING BECAUSE AS LONG AS YOUR FRIENDS HAVE YOUR BACK EVERYTHING IS GOING TO BE ALRIGHT, AND ANNA STOOD UP TO THE BULLY BECAUSE SHE KNEW IT WAS THE RIGHT THING TO DO AND DIEGO WAS BY HER SIDE EVERY STEP OF THE WAY. MEANWHILE THE CLASS ROOM WAS A COMPLETELY DIFFERENT STORY, IF ANNA WAS TO REVEAL DIEGO TO THE CLASS ROOM IT WAS ONLY OBVIOUS AS TO WHAT MIGHT HAPPEN AND SHE LOVED THE IDEA OF BRINGING HER NEW BEST FRIEND DIEGO TO SCHOOL WITH HER, IT MADE HER FEEL INVINCIBLE LIKE SHE COULD TAKE ON THE WORLD, HER AND DIEGO

THE FRIENDLY FORCE TO BE RECKONED WITH, SO ANNA HAD TO BE SUPER CAREFUL AT ALL TIMES . DIEGO SNUCK A NAP IN THE CLASS ROOM MOST DAYS WHILE THE KIDS PLAYED, BUT SHE HAD TO HIDE HIM AWAY FROM THE TEACHERS SIGHT WHICH WAS EASY BECAUSE THE TEACHER USUALLY SAT ON THE SOFA MOST OF THE TIME SIPPING HER COFFEE.

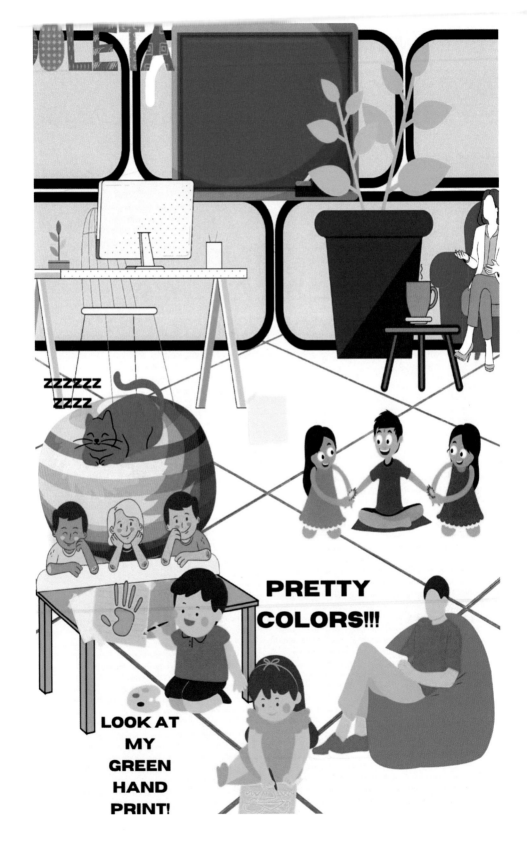

ANNA EVEN HAD TO HIDE DIEGO FROM HER GRANDMA AND LITTLE ANNA ALWAYS TOLD HER GRANDMA EVERYTHING, SHE TOLD HER GRANDMA ALL OF HER SECRETS AND STORIES, BUT NO NOT THIS TIME, DIEGO WAS WAY TOO PRECIOUS TO ANNA, SHE WANTED HIM TO HERSELF LIKE A HOT PIECE OF APPLE PIE THAT TASTE SO GOOD YOU JUST WANT IT ALL TO YOURSELF. NOW ANNA WASN'T MUCH FOR MAKING FRIENDS AT FIRST BECAUSE SHE WAS ALWAYS SO SHY WHICH WAS STRANGE BECAUSE SHE' WAS QUITE THE OPPOSITE AT HOME, AT HOME SHE WAS ALWAYS JUMPING AROUND LIKE A KANGAROO AND SWINGING ON THINGS LIKE A MONKEY, BUT LATELY SHE WANTED TO BE A KITTEN INSTEAD OF A MONKEY AND SHE STOPPED BEING SHY AT SCHOOL BUT INSTEAD SHE WAS SMILING ALL

OF THE TIME WITH NOT A WORRY IN THE WORLD , SHE EVEN MADE A FEW EXTRA FRIENDS AND THEY PLAYED WITH HER EVERY DAY AT LUNCH TIME , THERE NAMES WEAR CARMEN AND XAVIER, AND LET ME JUST SAY IT WAS SO NICE TO SEE ANNA SO HAPPY .

its raining its pooring the old man is snoring.

EVEN THOUGH ANNA HAD HID DIEGO FROM THE WORLD SHE SOON REALIZED SHE COULDN'T HIDE HIM FOREVER, SO SHE MADE A DECISION THAT COULD POSSIBLY DESTROY HER FRIENDSHIP WITH DIEGO FOREVER , SHE DECIDED TO SPILL THE APPLE SAUCE TO HER GRANDMA, ANNA TOLD HER GRANDMA ABOUT WHY SHE WANTED THE EXTRA LUNCHES AND THE EXTRA FOOD SHE NEEDED AND WHY HER BACKPACK WAS ALWAYS SO HEAVY , THINKING HER GRANDMA WOULDN'T BELIEVE HER, TO HER SURPRISE HER GRANDMA ACTUALLY DID BELIEVED HER, IN FACT SHE EVEN SHOWED ANNA HOW MUCH SHE BELIEVED HER BY LETTING DIEGO STAY AND TAKING BOTH OF THEM OUT FOR ICE CREAM, ANNA GAVE HER GRANDMA THE BIGGEST HUG IN THE WORLD AND RAN UPSTAIRS TO HER BEDROOM TO GET DIEGO ,BUT HE WAS

NOWHERE TO BE SEEN, SHE LOOKED UNDER HER BED IN THE CLOSET EVEN BEHIND HER PILLOWS AND UNDER HER BLANKETS BUT HE STILL WASN'T THERE . SHE COULD NOT BELIEVE IT, HER AND DIEGO NEVER LEAVE EACH OTHER'S SIDE, ANNA'S HEART DROPPED AND SHE BEGAN TO CRY OUT FOR DIEGO. HER GRANDMA COULDN'T BEAR TO SEE ANNA SO HEARTBROKEN, SO ANNA , HER TWO UNCLES AND GRANDMA GOT IN THE CAR AND WENT ON THE SEARCH THROUGH THE WHOLE NEIGHBORHOOD, MINUTES TURNED INTO HOURS AND SOON LIGHT TURNED TO DARK , IT WAS TIME TO GO BACK HOME AND UNFORTUNATELY WITHOUT DIEGO , ANNA WASN'T ABOUT TO GIVE UP THAT EASY THOUGH , HER BEST FRIEND WAS OUT THERE AND SHE WASN'T GOING TO FORGET HIM SO SHE

MADE ONE LAST DESPERATE ATTEMPT BY PUTTING UP MISSING FLYERS.

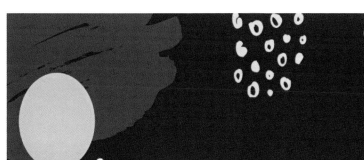

MISSING:

TREATS

HAVE YOU SEEN DIEGO

HELP US FIND OUR CAT PLEASE

SHE ONLY HAD THREE AND THE ODDS WERE AGAINST HER BUT ANNA KNEW A LITTLE HOPE GOES A LONG WAYS. EVEN IF THE ODDS ARE NOT IN YOUR FAVOR YOU STILL MUST TRY AND THAT'S WHAT THIS BRAVE LITTLE GIRL DID. ANNA WAS THAT TYPE OF PERSON THAT WHENEVER THINGS GOT TOUGH SHE ALWAYS LOOKED AT THE GOOD IN LIFE AND SHE ALWAYS HAD HOPE, AND WELL FOR HER AGE SHE WAS ONE SMART COOKIE AS WELL, I THINK SHE PICKED THAT TRAIT UP FROM A LITTLE OF EVERYONE IN THE FAMILY BUT ESPECIALLY FROM HER GRANDMA. NOW 3 DAYS WENT BY AND THERE WAS STILL NO SIGN OF DIEGO ANYWHERE AND ANNA'S BIRTHDAY WAS JUST AROUND THE CORNER , WE WERE ALL BEGINNING TO WORRY THAT HE WASN'T GOING TO COME BACK HOME AND WE KNEW IT WOULD

DEVASTATE ANNA IF WE DIDN'T FIND HIM BEFORE HER BIG DAY BECAUSE HE HAD BECOME A BIG PART OF HER LIFE , SHE NEEDED HER BEST FRIEND WITH HER SO WE DECIDED TO PUT DIEGO IN THE NEWSPAPER , AND FROM THERE ALL WE COULD DO IS WAIT FROM THEN ON OUT, THEN AFTER WAITING WHAT FELT LIKE MILLIONS OF YEARS ANNA WAS WOKEN BY A MEOW OUTSIDE OF HER BEDROOM WINDOW , SO SHE TIPTOAD OVER TO HER WINDOW AND GAVE A SLIGHT PEEK AND THERE HE WAS BUT NOT ALONE BUT WITH A WHITE KITTEN IN PINK.

I FOUND DEIGO
GRANDMA!!! WITH A
PRETTY KITTIE

ANNA COULDN'T BELIEVE WHAT SHE HAD FOUND, WITH EXCITEMENT SHE SLIPPED ON HER GOWN RAN DOWN STAIRS AND DANCED ALL AROUND, SHE HAD JUST FOUND DIEGO, SHE COULDN'T CONTAIN HERSELF, FILLED WITH SO MUCH EXCITEMENT ANNA YELLED AND SANG OUT LOUD, SHE PICKED DIEGO UP AND DANCED IN CIRCLES, THAN SHE CRIED BUT NOT THE TEARS YOU THINK, THESE TEARS WEREN'T JUST ANY OLD TEARS, THEY WERE HAPPY TEARS THAT SHE HAD FOUND HIM, PROMISE YOU WILL NEVER LEAVE AGAIN!!! ANNA WHISPERED TO DIEGO, MEOW, DIEGO PROMISED AS LONG AS HE COULD STILL SEE THE OTHER KITTEN NEXT DOOR.

IT TURNS OUT DIEGO NEVER EVEN LEFT, HE HAD A GIRL KITTEN HE LIKED RIGHT THERE NEXT DOOR THE WHOLE TIME, HE WAS JUST HANGING OUT WITH HER A LOT MORE AND OF ALL PLACES THE ROOF OF THE HOUSE, BUT WE COULDN'T BLAME HIM BECAUSE THAT'S WHERE THE MOST BEAUTIFUL VIEW IS. THE NEXT DAY IT WAS ANNA'S BIRTHDAY SO HER AND DIEGO HANDED OUT INVITATIONS TO ALL THE KIDS AT SCHOOL AND ANNA HAD A GOOD IDEA TO INVITE GARTH THE BULLY, SHE THOUGHT MAYBE IF SHE INVITED HIM THAN HE WOULD EASE UP ON HER AND DIEGO AND STOP BULLYING THEM AND HOPEFULLY DEVELOP A FRIENDSHIP OVER TIME, ANNA WAS A LITTLE NERVOUS AT FIRST TO ASK HIM BUT SHE SUCKED UP ENOUGH COURAGE AND WENT FOR IT, EXPECTING A SHOVE TO THE GROUND

GARTH INSTEAD EXCEPTED HER INVITE AND SMILED AT HER AND DIEGO, GARTH EVEN APOLOGIZED FOR THE HURTFUL THINGS HE SAID AND THE THINGS HE HAD DONE TO THEM BOTH AND ANNA AND DIEGO EXCEPTED HIS APOLOGY AND FROM THAT DAY ON HE BECAME A GOOD FRIEND TO THEM.

AND AS A FRIENDSHIP BUILT SO DID DIEGO'S LOVE FOR DELILAH THE WHITE KITTEN IN PINK NEXT DOOR, OH HOW TRUE LOVE AND TRUE FRIENDSHIPS WORK ,FULL OF LIFE AND FULL OF LOVE AND SO FULL OF WONDER , LIFE IS ACTUALLY SO FULL OF WONDER THAT SHORTLY AFTER DIEGO BECAME A PART OF OUR FAMILY SO DID A FEW OTHER REALLY COOL CATS AND THEIR NAMES ARE MR. COOL, HE IS A BIG ORANGE CAT WITH A LOT OF CLASS, THAT'S WHY HIS NAME IS MR. COOL BECAUSE HE IS A COOL CAT AND THEN THERE'S PRISSY , SHE IS A BLACK CAT AND SHE IS A LOVE BUG , BOTH MR COOL AND PRISSY ARE REALLY GOOD CATS AND THEY ARE ALSO REALLY GOOD FRIENDS JUST AS DIEGO IS BUT MOST OF ALL THEY ARE FAMILY.

EVEN THOUGH ALL THREE CATS WERE PART OF THE FAMILY DIEGO REMAINED THE SPECIAL ONE TO ANNA , MR. COOL WAS UNCLE AUSTIN'S CAT AND PRISSY WAS GRANDMAS CAT BUT DIEGO WAS ANNA'S AND THEY EXPLORED THE WILDERNESS TOGETHER.

ITS A BIRD, ITS A
PLANE

NO ITS A
HOT AIR
BALLOON

THEY EVEN WENT STAR WATCHING MOST NIGHTS IN THE WATER WITH NOT A CARE IN THE WORLD THIS WAS AN INSEPARABLE BOND THAT NO ONE OR THING COULD BREAK , ANNA AND DIEGO WERE THE BEST OF FRIENDS AND BOTH OF THEM NEEDED EACH OTHER IN THEIR LIFE'S AND IN THE END THEY BROUGHT OUT THE BEST IN ONE ANOTHER , SO REMEMBER FRIENDS COME AND FRIENDS GO BUT THE ONES THAT STAY MAY BE THAT CUTE FURRY FRIEND OF YOURS AT HOME ...THE END

Made in the USA
Columbia, SC
05 April 2021

35624392R00029